THE WILD WORLD OF ANIMALS

THE WILD WORLD OF ANIMALS

PARROTS

JILL KALZ

CREATIVE EDUCATION

Published by Creative Education, 123 South Broad Street, Mankato, Minnesota 56001. Creative Education is an imprint of The Creative Company. Designed by Rita Marshall. Production design by Advertising & Design, Inc. Photographs by Alamy (Advance Images, Juniors Bildarchiv, blickwinkel, Coral Planet, Danita Delimont, Huw Evans, david hancock, William Harvey, Byron Jorjorian, Christian Kapteyn, Kevin Schafer, Andre Seale, Steve Bloom Images, Stock Connection, Robert M. Vera, Dave Watts), Getty Images (The Bridgeman Art Library, Joel Sartore, Scotr Sroka, Pete Turner).
Printed in the United States of America. Library of Congress Cataloging-in-Publication Data: Kalz, Jill. Parrots / by Jill Kalz. p. cm. — (The wild world of animals). Includes bibliographical references. ISBN-13: 978-1-58341-434-7. 1. Parrots—Juvenile literature. I. Title. II. Wild world of animals (Creative Education). QL696.P7K354 2006 598.7'1—dc22 2005048230. First edition 9 8 7 6 5 4 3 2 1

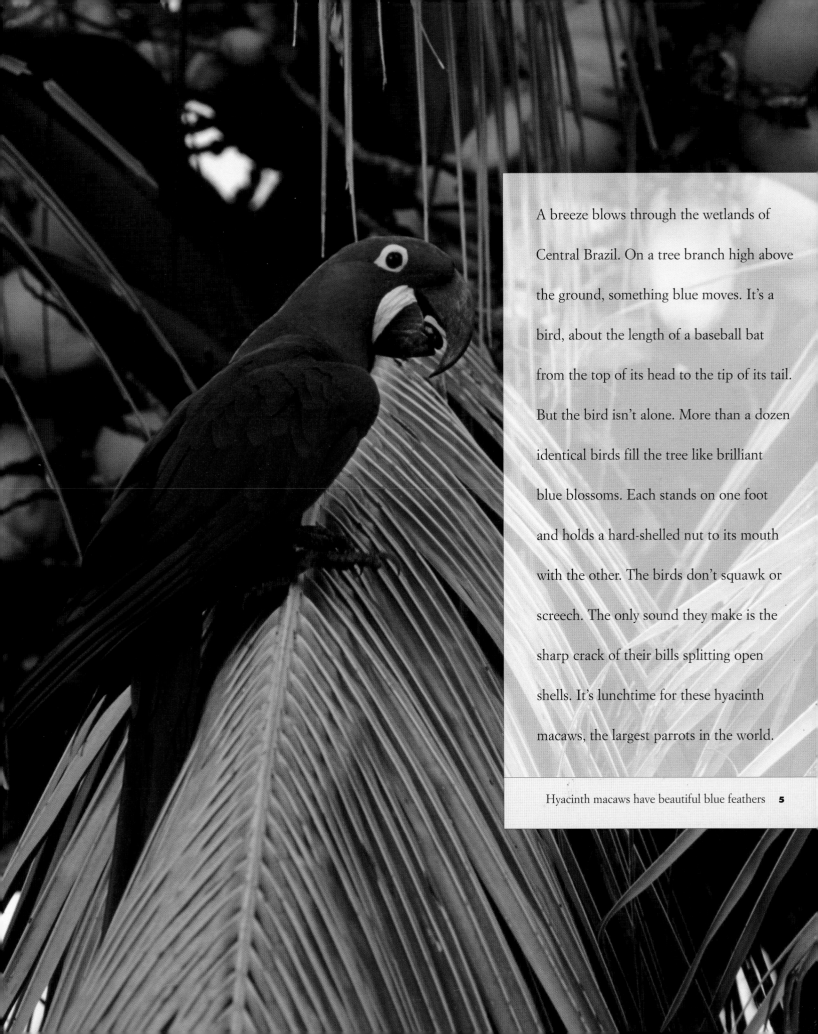

A breeze blows through the wetlands of Central Brazil. On a tree branch high above the ground, something blue moves. It's a bird, about the length of a baseball bat from the top of its head to the tip of its tail. But the bird isn't alone. More than a dozen identical birds fill the tree like brilliant blue blossoms. Each stands on one foot and holds a hard-shelled nut to its mouth with the other. The birds don't squawk or screech. The only sound they make is the sharp crack of their bills splitting open shells. It's lunchtime for these hyacinth macaws, the largest parrots in the world.

Hyacinth macaws have beautiful blue feathers **5**

WINGED JEWELS

The parrot family is made up of more than 350 **species**. Members include macaws, parakeets, cockatoos, and budgerigars. The scarlet macaw is perhaps the best-known. Parrots range in size from the 4-inch (10 cm) pygmy parrot of New Guinea to the 40-inch (102 cm) hyacinth macaw of Bolivia and Brazil. Parrots can weigh as little as a sparrow or as much as a newborn human baby.

6 Some macaws can be 35 inches (90 cm) in length

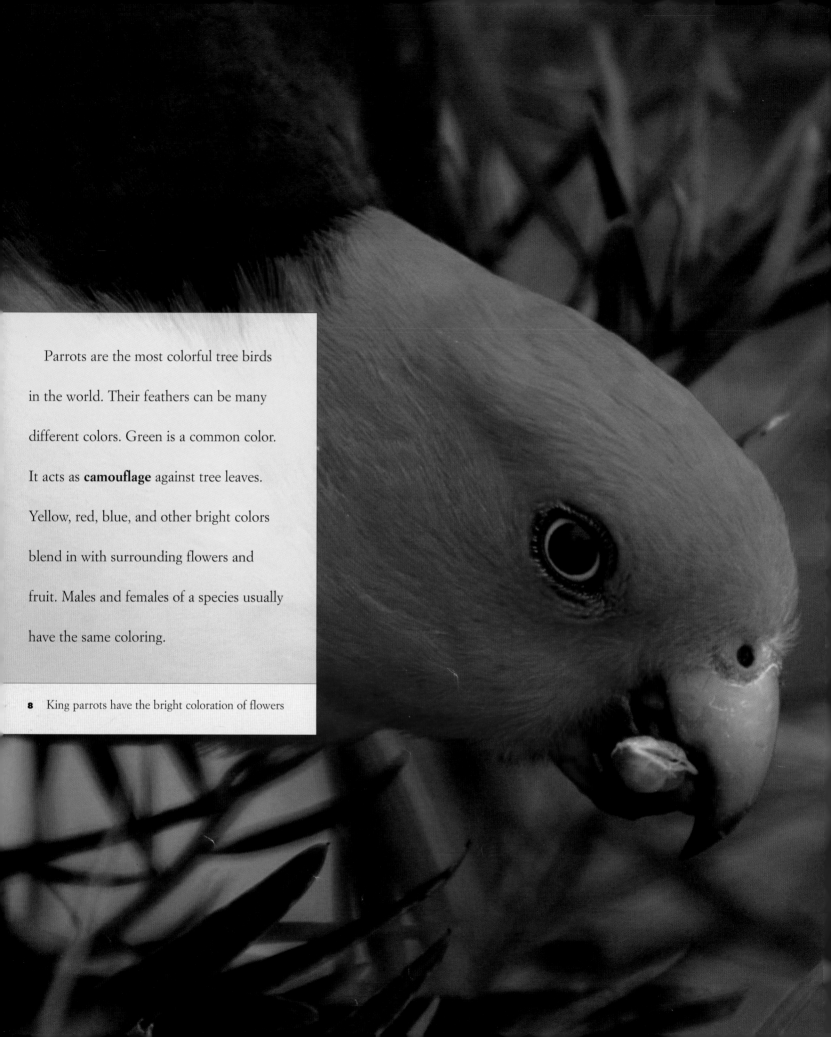

Parrots are the most colorful tree birds in the world. Their feathers can be many different colors. Green is a common color. It acts as **camouflage** against tree leaves. Yellow, red, blue, and other bright colors blend in with surrounding flowers and fruit. Males and females of a species usually have the same coloring.

8 King parrots have the bright coloration of flowers

Parrots live mostly in the **tropical** forests of
South America, Africa, and Asia. The weather
there is warm, and food is plentiful. Because
the jungle is so rich with life, parrots share
their **habitat** with many different animals.
Monkeys, snakes, and sloths climb through
the towering trees. Jaguars prowl below.
Eagles, owls, and hawks soar overhead.

Many parrots share the trees with monkeys   **9**

A few parrot species live in places other than tropical forests. Some live in the dry, open country of Australia. Some live in city parks and gardens in South Africa. Thick-billed parrots live in the pine forests of Mexico. One kind of parrot even lives in the snowy mountains of New Zealand.

10 New Zealand's kea is the only mountain parrot

Even though they come in many different sizes and colors, and live in different
places, all parrots share several common
traits. Parrots have a hooked bill that
is hinged on the top. The hinge allows
parrots to open their mouth very wide.
Parrots use their bill to eat, but they also
use it as a third foot. They climb trees by
grabbing branches with their bill and pull-
ing themselves up.

Parrots feel at home in a tree's topmost branches **11**

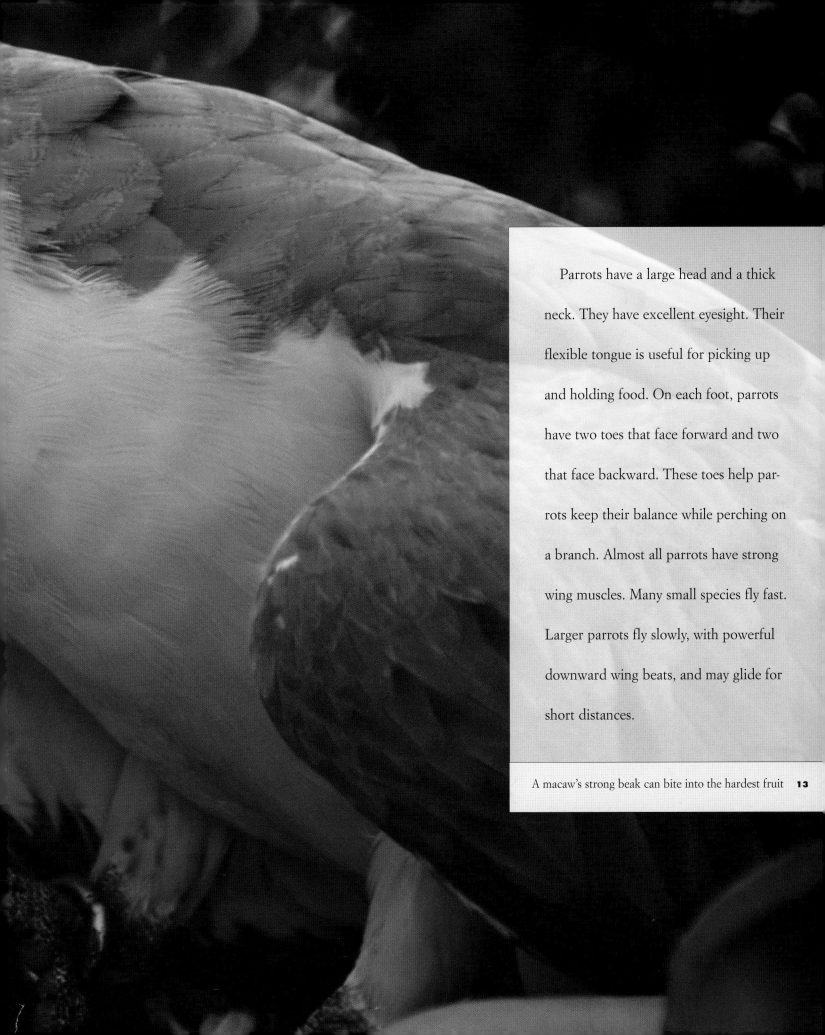

Parrots have a large head and a thick neck. They have excellent eyesight. Their flexible tongue is useful for picking up and holding food. On each foot, parrots have two toes that face forward and two that face backward. These toes help parrots keep their balance while perching on a branch. Almost all parrots have strong wing muscles. Many small species fly fast. Larger parrots fly slowly, with powerful downward wing beats, and may glide for short distances.

A macaw's strong beak can bite into the hardest fruit   **13**

LIFE AS A PARROT

❦

Parrots would rather be with other parrots than alone. Depending on the species, parrot flocks may include more than 100 birds. Large flocks help protect parrots from **predators**. It's hard for a jaguar or eagle to attack with 200 eyes watching!

Macaws often move in large flocks

Parrots spend most of their life in the trees. Mornings and early evenings are their active times, when the sun isn't so hot. During the day, parrots eat, fly, and play with other parrots in the flock. At night, they sleep huddled together. Parrots love to make noise. They communicate with each other with squawks, shrieks, and whistles. Unlike pet parrots, wild parrots do not **mimic** the sounds around them.

Parrots are among the most intelligent of all birds **15**

Most parrots eat seeds, fruits, and nuts. Parrots eat slowly and quietly. They stand on one foot and hold the food up to their bill with the other. Parrots are the only birds that eat this way.

16 A parrot's feet are both strong and flexible

When they're not eating or napping, parrots are **preening**. Like all birds, parrots have contour feathers (the outer feathers) for flying and down feathers (the layer of soft, fluffy feathers underneath) to keep warm. But they also have powder-down feathers.

Powder-down feathers break apart easily into a fine powder. Parrots use this powder to shine their contour feathers. Once a year, parrots **molt**. They lose just a few feathers at a time, rather than all of them at once, so they are always able to fly.

18   Parrots spend a lot of time preening themselves

When a parrot is between two and four years old, it looks for a partner to mate with. Parrots mate for life, which means they stay together until one of them dies. Most parrots don't build a nest. Some lay their eggs in existing tree holes. Others carve nesting holes in termite mounds or canyon walls. Depending on the species, a female parrot lays two to six eggs and **incubates** them.

Some parrots are very affectionate with their mates

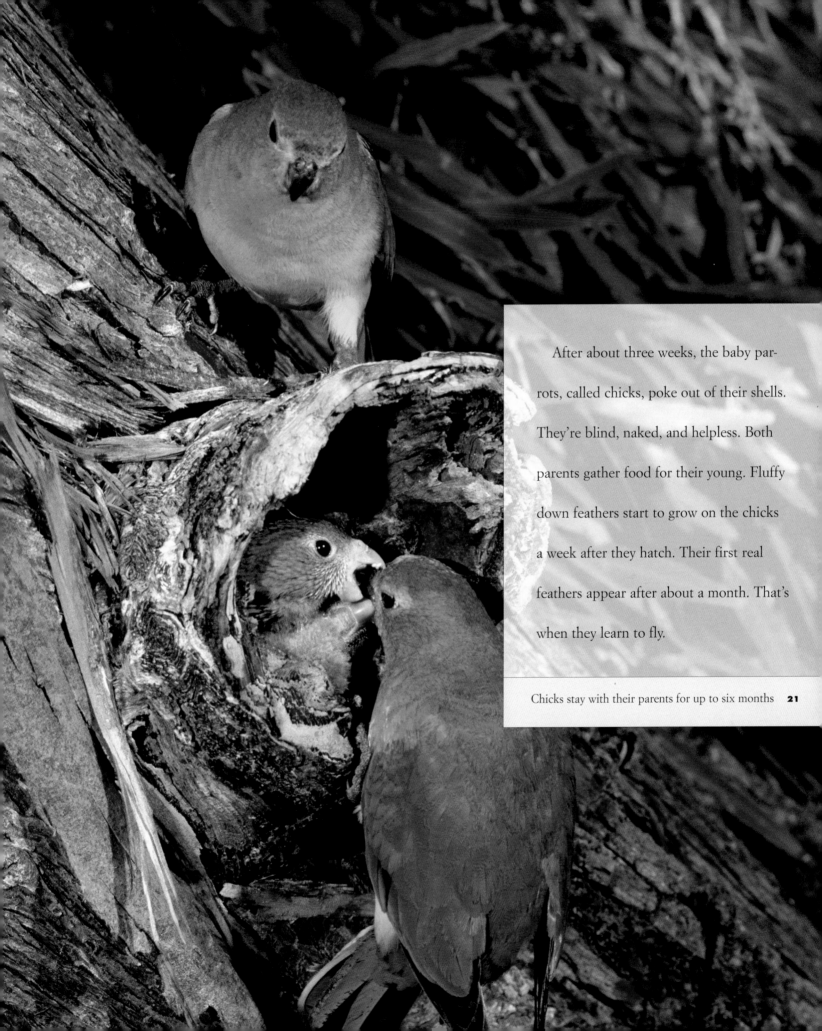

After about three weeks, the baby parrots, called chicks, poke out of their shells. They're blind, naked, and helpless. Both parents gather food for their young. Fluffy down feathers start to grow on the chicks a week after they hatch. Their first real feathers appear after about a month. That's when they learn to fly.

Chicks stay with their parents for up to six months **21**

Larger parrots live longer than smaller

parrots. A budgerigar, one of the smallest

parrots, has a life span of about 10 years.

Macaws, on the other hand, live an average

of 50 years in the wild.

Parrots have longer lives than most other birds

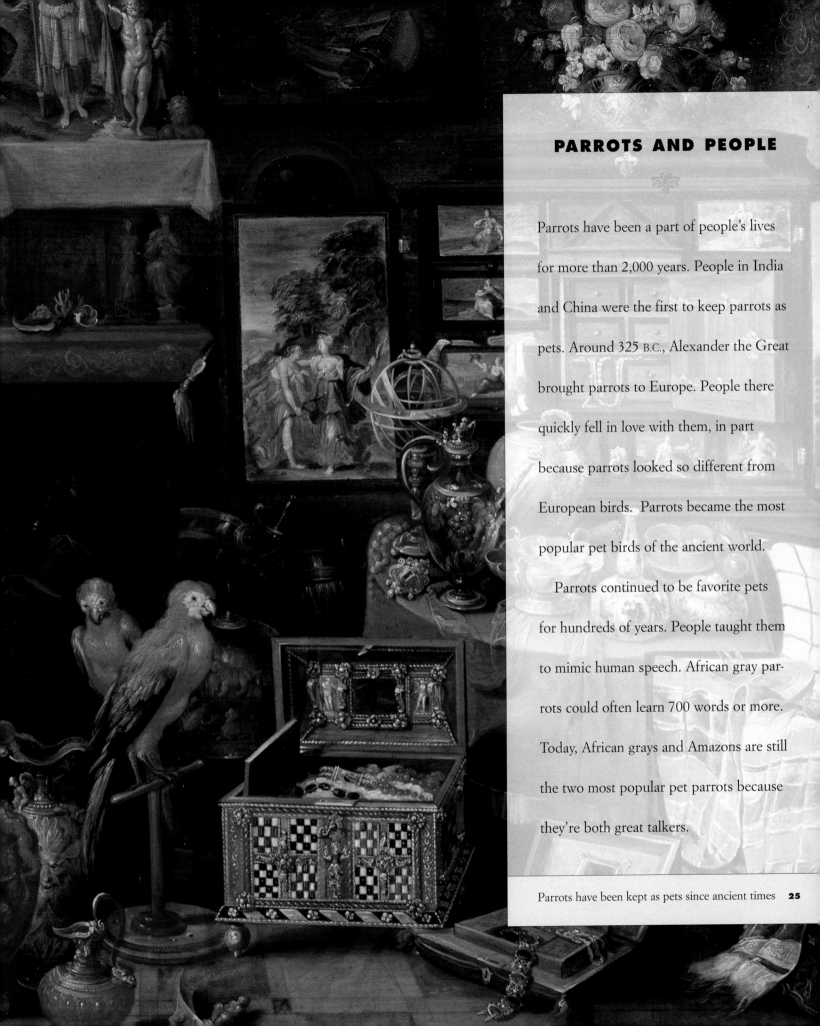

PARROTS AND PEOPLE

Parrots have been a part of people's lives for more than 2,000 years. People in India and China were the first to keep parrots as pets. Around 325 B.C., Alexander the Great brought parrots to Europe. People there quickly fell in love with them, in part because parrots looked so different from European birds. Parrots became the most popular pet birds of the ancient world.

Parrots continued to be favorite pets for hundreds of years. People taught them to mimic human speech. African gray parrots could often learn 700 words or more. Today, African grays and Amazons are still the two most popular pet parrots because they're both great talkers.

Parrots have been kept as pets since ancient times **25**

In the 1700s, people wanted parrots for a different reason: feathers. They covered capes and dresses with colorful parrot feathers. They made feather fans and scarves. Some women even wore stuffed birds on their hats.

This fashion trend lasted until the early 1900s. Millions of parrots were killed each year. Eventually, some species became **extinct**. Laws were passed to limit the use of feathers for fashion and decoration. But parrots faced other threats to their survival.

Parrot feathers used to be made into garments **27**

As the world's population grew, people cleared trees away to make room for roads, houses, and farmland. Many parrots soon had no place to live and no food to eat. If they tried to eat farmers' crops, they were either shot or poisoned. Luckily, many countries around the world now have laws that make it illegal to kill parrots.

Today, people who want to keep parrots as pets may be the birds' biggest threat. Some

Many parrots today are at risk of becoming extinct

people cut down nesting trees, hoping to sell the chicks they find. Many newly hatched parrots die as the trees fall to the ground. Many more parrots die in their cages during the long journey to other countries. It is illegal to sell certain parrot species, but some people do it anyway. They can make a lot of money by selling parrots. A hyacinth macaw, for example, can bring up to $12,000.

Only about 5,000 hyacinth macaws remain in the wild **29**

Even though some parrot species are gone forever, the future for parrots looks hopeful. Many people around the world are now working hard to protect parrots and their habitats. With everyone's help, parrots will continue to fill the air with their colorful wings and noisy squawks for a long time to come.

Macaws are loud, curious, and colorful creatures

GLOSSARY

Camouflage is coloring that helps make an animal hard to see in its surroundings.

When the last of a certain kind of plant or animal dies, we say it has become **extinct**.

The place where a creature lives is called its **habitat**.

When a bird **incubates** an egg, it keeps it warm so the new bird inside can grow.

To **mimic** is to copy or imitate how something looks and acts.

When animals **molt**, they shed old fur or feathers to make room for new fur or feathers.

Predators are animals that kill and eat other animals.

When a bird is cleaning and straightening its feathers, it is **preening** itself.

Some animals are divided into different kinds, or **species**. Members of a species can have young together.

Traits are features or characteristics.

If something is **tropical**, it can be found in warm parts of the world, near the equator.

BOOKS

Altman, Linda Jacobs. *Parrots*. New York: Benchmark Books/Marshall Cavendish, 2001.

Parrots. Milwaukee, Wis.: Gareth Stevens Publishing, 2004.

Rauzon, Mark J. *Parrots Around the World*. New York: Franklin Watts, 2001.

WEB SITES

Animal Bytes: Macaw http://www.sandiegozoo.org/animalbytes/t-macaw.html

Cockatoo Birds http://www.cockatoo-birds.com

Parrots International http://www.parrotsinternational.org

INDEX